paper girl
AND THE
knives that Made her

ARI B. COFER

central
avenue
PUBLISHING

2022

Published by Central Avenue Publishing, an imprint of Central Avenue Marketing Ltd.
www.centralavenuepublishing.com

PAPER GIRL AND THE KNIVES THAT MADE HER

Trade Paperback: 978-1-77168-264-0
Ebook: 978-1-77168-265-7

Published in Canada
Printed in United States of America

1. POETRY / African American & Black   2. POETRY / Women Authors

10 9 8 7 6 5 4 3 2 1

to my friends,
who have always listened to my stories

to gerald,
who helped me stay alive
to see the end of this chapter

this collection comes with
the following content warnings.
please be safe.
read at a healthy pace.
talk with your loved ones.
take what you need.
leave the rest.

mental health conditions
suicide/suicidal ideation
self-harm
sexual assault
gun violence
violence against poc
brief mentions of body dysmorphia
brief mentions of drug/alcohol use
+ other tough topics

preface

i have never been anything
but a paper girl.
something to tear into pieces.

something to burn.

<u>preface (ii)</u>

paper girls
can cut back.

longing and the tenderness that frays you

(is the grief more painful than the wanting?)

a world with no bottom

the way the sky crawls over the sea
the way what's big will always smother
the way we sprint after our breath
the way there is no overtaking what empties us
the way all roads lead back to the tearstained bathtub in your
mother's house
the way the floorboards are stained from how it always spills over
the way the taste of your becomings is always behind your tongue
the way your throat is cracked from trying to spit the old you out
the way you cut your teeth on homing shadows
the way the darkness has followed you ever since
the way tomorrow grips you
the way you have never let go
the way nothing
ever
really
ends

<u>my chest is full</u>

i was told to write about you
in less than five lines
and i am once again reminded
how much space
you take up

picasso

you created a version
of me that carved away
my insides
and painted my heart
a bruised clock.

parts of me scattered on the canvas.
i have become less
home to love and more
shell to fill
and i can't forgive you for
turning me into another memory to frame
on your wall of
paper girls.

i don't know if i should call you
an artist or
a butcher,

but either way
i'm empty now.

the fairy tale becomes a memory

now that you're gone,
i reach inside my chest
to cling to the pieces of you that made
a home inside me.

i hold my breath
because i'm afraid of losing what's left of you
in an exhale.

now that you're gone,
my face is wrinkled from clenching my eyes shut
to try to get a glimpse of your memory.
to see the way you left me.

they always say the best way to move on
is to go through,
but i didn't know i would ever have to
do this without you.
not knowing what could be is worse than
remembering what was.

all this to say, i miss you. and i don't know why forever wasn't in
our story.
but i'll reread the old chapters anyway just to pretend, if only for
a moment,

we got our ever after.

heartbreak survival guide

1. it's going to get worse. it's going to get worse. it's going to feel like they left you all over again every time you *inhale. exhale. inhale.* they're still gone. they're still gone. they're still gone.

2. don't reread the love letters. don't burn them either. they're your grandchild's first fairy tale. an instruction guide to your next lover. a reminder that you survived.

3. you'll regret texting them if you do. *i miss you* only sounds like song lyrics when there's music playing. they are a badly strung violin.

4. tell everyone. don't hide your broken. shout from the rooftops that you're bleeding. get emergency surgery. resuscitate in 3-2-1 . . . detach yourself from the burden of silence. they did not take your voice when they left.

5. remember the clichés. it will pass. this is the hardest part. nothing lasts forever. sit in your lonely and make a crown out of it. deem yourself royalty and look into a mirror. look at your kingdom. you built this body. no person can crumble it. fill in the cracks. start again.

<u>home</u>

the midwest held nothing but tornadoes, blizzards,
and you.
each one of those took the breath out of me.
left my heart homeless.
left me digging through the wreckage
trying to find a way out of this mess.
left me realizing there was no way to take the girl out of the
disaster that made her.

but still, i find myself admitting
i would do it over and over and over again.
i would take shelter every day if it meant
getting to spend another second
in the country
with you.

(3) missed calls

hey, it's me. which, that's obvious, but since i'm having a hard time remembering what your voice sounds like, maybe you've forgotten the sound of mine? anyway, i called to tell you i still wear your new york t-shirt sometimes. my new lover says i must love new york, and i say no, i love the people. i have the journal you gave me too. i wrote our last conversation in it. i wrote one word to a page to help it last a little longer. i'm rambling now. i called because i walked by a man who smelled like you. or maybe it was your ghost. either way can you call me back? i promise i'll answer this time.

sacrifices

i would bleed out for you over and over again.
i know it's not healthy, but i would.
i would empty my veins to show you there's room for you here in
my body.
a place we call sanctuary.

we become martyrs because
there is always something bigger to believe in.

i wish i had known that before
i followed you.

prayers for a gone girl

i am restless for the way you want me. i don't know how else to
say this, but to wrap it around your throat and choke you with it.
and i don't mean to be rough, but my mother always said the best
way to ripen a lemon was to apply pressure. that holding on tight
meant they were just too afraid to lose what's left. i want you,
i want you, i want you, but you keep saying that yearning for a
disappearing act is the most violent suicide. that you cannot keep
wanting a girl who dances with a reaper or a lover who does not
hold herself at the end of a long night.

and i'm sorry. i know i am screaming to you from the grave. you
cannot hear me if i am a ghost. me wanting to end my life
makes you crave a world in which you never knew a sad girl to
begin with.

all this to say, i love you. i really fucking love you. my brain is
my heart's cancer and i dissolve into myself when you say my
name. and i know it's there when you fall asleep. the version of
us you've always wanted us to be. seeing every thunderstorm
as a reason to take shelter inside each other's stomach. making
friends with the butterflies.

i just need you to admit that you want me, want me, want me. and
i don't want you to blame it on the yearning.

two truths and a lie:

1. certain birds remind me of the way you'd sing. a low hymn that got faster as you smiled through tomorrow's melodies.
2. i don't like birds anymore. they're loud and bothersome and don't know when to stop singing, singing, singing. they're awful communicators when you think about it.
3. i'm happier outside of this birdcage we called home.

I WISH YOU WEREN'T
THE SONG THAT
LED ME HOME.

before i close my eyes

i think about how we are both paper
but i was the one who got the cuts.

i think about how you left coffee stains on my hands
because you never learned how to clean a mess.

i think about your goodbye and how it sounded
like a gunshot.
i think about how i've been bleeding ever since.

i think about you and i crumble.
you are forevermore sketched in the darkness.

before i close my eyes
i pray to see anything

but

you.

<u>let's unpack this</u>

when i saw you walk away,
i didn't realize you had so much of me
buried within your baggage.

it's no wonder i haven't been able to
find those parts of me since.

<u>dead things</u>

i buried our love today.
took a shovel and dug 12 feet—
6 for my heart and
6 for your hands,
and what a wicked ceremony
a funeral is.
taking dead forevers
and drowning them underground;

i plan on visiting the cemetery.
waiting for ghosts to guide me down
under.
waiting for daisies to push out of our
yesterdays.
robbing our grave of the valuable parts of
our love.

i have been so haunted since we became dead things.
when will the sorrow be
enough?

about us

watching the storm roll in and leaving the raincoat on the kitchen
counter and building sandcastles on the shoreline and running,
running, running down a forked road and tying a bow tie loose
enough to keep breathing and believing the sun is too beautiful
a thing to let me burn and pulling out every beaming thing from
the soil before letting them bloom
and leaving
and leaving
and leaving
and
this is the way
i loved you

the undoing before the fray

outside my house on west russet grove circle,
dylan tells me his father caught him sneaking a cigarette and
made him drag the whole pack.
he is the first boy to give me second-hand smoke.

we are 11 and racing to meet our friends at the playground. he
tells me of all the other treacherous things he has done.

(used the backyard hose and his mother's dove bar to drown the
expletives.)
(pillaged the porn stash hidden in his father's shoe boxes.)

do you want to see them?

and i don't.
but now we are at the swing set and jared and corey are there.
i imagine they have been waiting for the opening.

why, are you scared?

and i am. the boys all know.
jared says he macgyvered a fort in the trees behind the zip
line. we disappear into the leaves because they all want their
turn with the paper girl. to rip the pages and build a bonfire.
to clear the smoke before their fathers tell them the only way
to taste adulthood is to swallow it whole. to call it a victory if
they have a mouthful before their molars sprout.

i draw a picture in my diary of a girl in the woodlands
surrounded by the neighborhood boys. i draw how they
showed her pictures of what she would eventually be. all
centerfold and fading. spread like breakfast jam. eyes begging
for more, *more*. bookmarked corners that helped the holder.
hurt the holding.

i write a confession about how it could've been much worse.
that i was barely budding with no fruit to take. that it's okay if
they searched anyway.

ten years later, dylan's sister posts that he has died. and it's
not from smoking or cursing or choking. it's from an accident
no one saw coming through the thick of the trees. she says she
is sad and sick and breathless. i want to tell her i understand.

second-hand smoke will find a way to do that to you.

<u>i saw their wedding photos on facebook</u>

you know, he probably doesn't even think about it anymore?
like, honestly, he has someone new – did you know they're
married? that he's married now? can you believe it? do you think
his wife – god, his wife – knows what he did to me? that her
flame is actually a wolf? that his cobalt eyes glow in the dark?
that he's hungry, really fucking hungry, and his teeth are stained
fangs? but see, if i were to come out and call her husband for
what he is – for what he did – would i be the bad guy? breaking
up white picket daydreams of a man and a woman playing
house? is ripping a man from a dream any less painful than a
man throwing me into a nightmare? would i be victim enough
then? would i be survivor enough yet? could i, finally, call him
what he is?

LOCAL MAN PILLAGES SANCTUARY, TAKES WHAT'S LEFT OF GIRL INSIDE

ISSUE #2

"HE DIDN'T KILL ME
BUT I WISH HE HAD,"
SHE SAID.

"THE DEVIL HAS
FOUND A WAY TO
MAKE THIS BODY
FEEL LIKE IT WILL
NEVER AGAIN
BE HOLY."

i think of the moon when i come

hear me out.

the first time i ever broke in a mattress,
i was at that super 8 off the interstate.
my mom told me those places had bed lice,
and my dad told me
they only had men looking for prey.
and there i was, sleepwalking into a bear's den. i was suicidal,
after all,
so i was always looking for opportunities for something
to swallow me
whole.
our room had shitty curtains that
couldn't close.
if you looked out the window
you could see the cars on the highway
all stuck,
brake lights making the whole world wait.
and oh, the irony of a boy driving me into the cotton sheets while
the universe outside was at
a standstill.
i looked out the window
from the bed
and watched the sky. the moon was out,
and it had the type of glow you wanted to
remember on a bad day.
i wondered if the moon
understood.
questioned how something as big as her

could get trapped in the orbit of what's bigger.
how she could somehow call it home anyway.
i asked her,
do you come every time the earth asks?
she said,
you learn very quickly that sometimes,
there is no other way out of this.

<u>i cried listening to olivia rodrigo's *drivers license* today</u>

you turned 16 before me.
your parents got you a white car
and you loved to drive me around the city like we were on the
run.
truth be told, loving each other was the worst crime we ever
committed.
villains hiding from who we were when the world wasn't moving.
windows down, hands out the sunroof.
if i were big enough, i would've reached for the sun and grabbed
it for you.
i would've let it burn my hands raw if it meant getting to hold this
feeling a little longer.
i gave you all the control as
i sat in the passenger's seat.
i would've let you crash the car if it meant
doing something with you that left an impact.

i hate remembering how we used to be because
i didn't know we would grow up one day.
that the imprint of your hand would fade off my thigh like the
best kind of scar.
i'm still healing from the way you would say
look, it doesn't matter where we're going as long as we get there
together.
every time i see a white car i understand forevers can only exist in
moments.
and i would do anything to hand you the keys again.

<u>church</u>

i have been praying
for your love,

but the way you treat me
is not holy.

the way i'm drowning in your absence
isn't a baptism.

you have never been a savior.

<u>when the well ran dry</u>

you drank from my veins and
with a breath, i went from
the whole ocean to
the biggest desert you've ever seen.

this is to say it only takes a moment to drain the love.
to take it all to keep
but never give.
i've been crawling in the dust of myself
trying to rebuild a home
but keep sinking in the sand.

i wish you didn't have to take so much from me.
i tried to give as much as i could.

<u>in an alternate universe</u>

i am so tired
i need you to understand
i can't do this anymore
the dark is pulling me in
please, don't try to save me
i'm ready to go

i want to keep trying
i know you see me now
living is honey and fruit
the light haloes me
i still need you here
it's not too late to stay

friday night lights

i was 15 the first time
i heard the echo of mournings
a bullet could make
after one lured my classmate
into an instant grave.
he had my pastor's name
and 16 years of practice
praying for a better tomorrow.
for not seeing a demon again.

i was an easy target
catching bullets
and hoping no one else
would ever want the gun.

        it was a tuesday when
        the world got 150 pounds lighter.

i'm still leaving gunpowder
fingerprints in the mirror
as if i pulled the trigger myself
because i was not fast enough to save him.

1̲7̲

the nights with too much whiskey / my hand in your hair / the way your parents knew my favorite meal / midnight drives to the abandoned asylum / looking for ghosts in everything we touch / trying not to disappear ourselves / realizing rain isn't magic but it can make you feel bewitched / kissing / *kissing you* / getting so close to fucking i could've sworn we did / the moon-filled street / sneaking out / sneaking in / the rain again / tracing scars / making scars / blue as a color and a feeling / realizing i am my home / i am my home / i am my home

magic

i've been on antidepressants since i was 15 and to me
pills work like magic tricks
in a count of
1, 2, 3,
your depression will vanish from your
heart and into your hands
where it can be seen
and not felt

and magic is funny that way. it's an illusion, meaning as long
as the audience is watching and believes my depression has
vanished,

it worked.

but every magic trick has its risks.

> *unintentional side effects of antidepressants include:*
> * *drowsiness*
> * *nausea*
> * *light-headedness*
> * *anxiety, and*
> * *suicidal thoughts*

so, while magic is a beautiful thing
sometimes it finds a way of hurting you in the process

but you keep doing magic.
keep performing tricks until your hands bleed
because you'd rather perform a vanishing act than become one.

i met a boy when i was 18.
i didn't tell him i was a closet magician because my type of magic tricks
were only meant to be performed in the dark.

he was about 10 years older than me and i thought it meant i
would be safe in his hands because

> *unintended side effects of antidepressants include:*
> • *impaired judgment*

i got in his car. he drove me to a parking lot i later learned would
act more like a cemetery
where he would bury his dead things.

he reached for my carcass.

and i tried to become a ghost in
1, 2, 3,
but sometimes magic tricks don't work if the audience isn't
paying attention.

i don't need to describe what happened next.

the only way i can say
> *i have been raped*
is in a poem,
because poems are like magic,
and magic is not real,
and maybe if i say
> *i have been raped*
enough times in a stanza,
i can convince myself that it was just another magic trick

another piece of wool pulled over my eyes
another thing i can explain
but not replicate
another thing that was never real to begin with.

> *unintended side effects of sexual assault include:*
> * *feeling like a stranger in your own body*
> * *flashbacks*
> * *nightmares*
> * *wondering if there is a universe where you won't see*
>   *their face in every man you meet*

so welcome to my magic show.
for my first act,
i'll keep swallowing pills until i can move my
pain from my heart and into my hands,

i will show it to you.
i'll fake happiness because
that's what survivors do,
i won't reveal how the trick is performed.
i can't show you what hides behind the curtains because you
might run and tell
the town about the fraud i am because

depression is in my mind.
the assault was a blurred line.

it's all fake.
      right?

remembering

muscle memory is:

       sinking when I hear your name
           forgetting how to swim
                breathing anyway

rest in pieces

sex should not be earned
or forced
or taken.

sex should be wanted
and freeing
and given.

i do not want to feel at war
every time i'm in bed.

headboards should not
feel like gravestones.

do not lay me to rest.
i'm tired of burying
this feeling.

<u>preparing for the viewing</u>

seeing a dead body
isn't as theatrical as it may seem.

it's almost as if you're 8 years old again,
walking into your mother's room to wake her up on a sunday
morning.
a person never looks more vulnerable
than when they are

still,
      eyes closed,
            begging for a moment more to be.

so, yeah, dead bodies don't scare me.

i saw my great-grandmother's in a beautifully flowered casket
during the first
shower of spring.
i saw some man's, mangled between the pavement and what used
to be a motorcycle.
i saw my great-uncle's, well, almost.
he wasn't quite dead yet, but i could tell there wasn't much left.
i learned young that life ends
when the desire goes,
and there's not much to desire when there's nowhere left to go.

i usually don't think of them,
but for some reason,
more bodies have been crowding

my home lately.
i am a cemetery to all of my losses.
i can only hold so many souls
in my chest before
i am left haunted.
before it buries me in grief.

i tell my therapist about these skeletons taking up all the open
seats in my living room.
she asks me if i remember when i had my first haunting and i say
easy, last april.
she asks me how i knew i had seen a dead thing, and i say
easy, you can push away the living but
you cannot lift the dead off your chest.
she asks me to say more and i say
no, i don't want to.
she asks if i see him now, and i tell her
i can see him all the time. i have seen the
dead before but i didn't know that some
still had beating hearts. had great-
grandmothers. had motorcycles. great uncles.
she asks me what i am feeling in my body and i tell her
i feel him. he is hot, and sweaty, and it is
loud. the room is filled with other bodies
and they all watch. they love a good
funeral. i cry my own eulogy. i
understand how god has created a world
with so many corpses. he is just another
man who loves the way a body breaks.
i tell her
i died that night on that couch. i knew i'd
been sent to hell when i woke up and his

body was still on top of mine. i have
tried to be alive again but i know it's all
fake. it will always be fake. i am always
pretending this didn't crucify me.

so like i said, seeing a dead body isn't theatrics.

it is the most intimate thing you will ever know.
you will learn to recognize them everywhere.
somehow i am able to
wake up every morning and
float through a graveyard.
i can name every ghoul
that has ever latched himself
inside of me.
i don't think the bodies will ever go away.

i even see one when i look in the mirror.

sculpted

the world thinks
trauma has turned me into
a work of art.

all it has done
is mold me into the stereotype
of a victim.

who am i, if not anything worth keeping?

a rhyme to distract you

i tried counting the number of scars on my
thigh but i lost count after 82.
and i wondered how many of those
thin white lines you had to cross before
i began dedicating them all to you.

i don't want to give you the pleasure of reading your name
after amy kay

dude is almost 30 years old when he matches with 18-year-old me
on tinder.
dude has brown hair and blue eyes.

dude asks if it's okay if we hang out. dude shows me around my
campus, telling me about his glory days as a student.
(dude never finished college.)
dude sits next to me on the bench and says he wants to hold my
hand.
dude holds my hand
even though i don't answer.

dude drives me back to my dorm. dude breaks the silence by
sucking his teeth. dude tells me what he wants me to do to him.
dude grabs my hand and puts it on his—

dude wants to hang out longer and i don't know how to say no.
dude drives me in circles. dude's wintry hands find their way to
where my thigh meets my inseam. dude doesn't ask. dude never
asks.
dude pulls over in the crossfit parking lot.
dude turns off his headlights because he wants to keep me in the
dark.
dude asks if i'm a virgin, and believes me when i lie and say i am.
dude sees an invitation.

dude doesn't hear me say "wait."
dude pulls me over the center console

onto his lap.
dude doesn't feel me pushing back.
dude has to see me pushing back.

dude doesn't realize he's the antagonist.
dude doesn't hear me say stop.
dude doesn't hear anything.
dude keeps going.

dude dropped me off at my dorm
and told me i was beautiful.
dude is the reason i can't tell the difference between *making love*
and *being fucked,*

dude doesn't know i now think being fucked is what it takes to be
loved,
dude never really knew me.

he just knew how to take what was left.

<u>what's left?</u>

i have emptied my cup
for men who take
yet somehow
i am the only one
drowning

<u>make your bed</u>

disheveled bedsheets and
crumpled, mismatched pillowcases
look the same way corey's bed
looked in elementary school.

we played video games
atop wrinkles and crumbs
and

you'd think it would feel
familiar years later when
i'm tossed onto messiness,
body crumpled with the comforter.

pillows feel more like bullet casings.
there is nothing familiar about
this feeling.

<u>haunted</u>

you were the first dead thing
that tried to make me
a corpse.

i wish you would stay in the ground.

<u>not a love poem</u>

your touch feels infinite.
a cosmic amount of tomorrows
graces my skin when you touch it;

his touch feels infinite.
i have spent too many yesterdays
trying to forget his grip;

this feeling is infinite.
there will be people who trace you
and they will linger for eternity:

i don't have
enough time
to feel this much.

<u>new girl</u>

when you find out your attacker has a new girlfriend,
you will feel guilty.

you will remember all the ways he touched you and wonder if his
sandpaper palms are causing her skin to break,

you will feel empty.

you'll be reminded of how he filled you up
and drained you all at once.

you will feel the abuse all over again.
you will feel how he treated your body like
the worst kind of meal,

a hungry-eyed wolf
with a palate just for you,

you will feel tired.

you will remember how hard it was to walk back home,
to take a shower,
to wash off the blood;

you will feel confused.
you'll wonder *was it really rape*
if i didn't report it?
you'll remember you didn't report it.

you'll tell yourself this girl would not be
in his claws
if you'd had the strength to rip off his nails,

you will remind yourself it's not your fault.

you did not choose to be raped,
the rapist chose to be a rapist,

you'll remind yourself to let go.

that women are strong beings,
and hope she's found a safe place in him,
and if not,
that she's finding an escape.

and you'll remind yourself you're not in that situation anymore.
you'll remember you are not traumatized,
you have trauma.

you'll get off the internet.
you'll self-soothe.
you'll forgive yourself.
you'll remind yourself you are safe.
and someday,
she will be too.

you
didn't want it
&
that should've
mattered.

good girl

you're not like other girls,
he says. he's got a blunt in his mouth
i was all too willing to hit and
that made me cool enough for him
to slide next to:

you're not like other girls,
he says. he's got a magnum in his hand
i was all too willing to put on and
that made me important enough for him
to slide into:
he runs his fingers through my hair,
whispers "good girl" into my ear.

       i have never known a good boy.

the only time i would ever call something a "good boy"
was if i was expecting it to bark back at me
but honestly, what's the difference between a man and a dog?
always jumping on its hind legs for fresh meat
running after things trying to get away
ripping apart good things at the seams—

this is not to say i hate dogs.
after all, i am not like other girls.
i am a good girl.
i am your girl dog.
i am your *bitch*.
obedient when you're looking for a quick bone,

but quick to attack the first person
to cross your path,

but i am tired of being on such a short leash.
i am so much more than a "good girl."
i am a kind girl.
i am a sexy girl.
i am a picky girl.
i am a strong girl.
i am a tired girl.
i am so fucking tired.
i am tired of loving a man so hard that i let him do whatever he
wants to my body.
i am tired of wanting validation so badly that i forget i am a
fucking queen—

and i am a queen.
men have so often brought me down
to my knees
where i am begging for mercy
but it's time for me to get up.
to brush the dirt off my legs
and realize
my voice will never be heard
if it's coming from the ground

and
i am not like other girls.
i am a mean girl.
i have skeletons in my closet
of the men who thought
i was too gentle to rip the flesh from their bones.

i am a cursed girl.
i am the witch who will call in her coven to send you
to the depths of hell.
i am a fierce girl,
i will hold you down by the throat
until you beg for this
good girl to become a
forgiving girl.

you're not like other girls,
he says.
he raises his hand to touch me
and i raise a fist,
both in solidarity and in power
that no man will ever
treat me like a bitch
again.

he puts his hand down.
and i say:
"good boy."

grief and the girl who soaks in it

(when will the sadness crumble?)

with an inhale, the wanting said,

are you sure you're ready for the end?

with an exhale, the grief said,

there's nothing left for me here.

ari b. cofer

<u>what do you think the birds are saying when they sing?</u>

i'm not quite sure if they're singing, darling.
i think they're mourning.
don't you know what it's like to feel sadness so heavy in your
chest, all you can do is exhale? yell? hum?
that's what they're doing.
i wish i knew a world where the line between screaming and
singing wasn't blurred,
but hasn't pain always kind of masked itself as pleasure?

anyway, let them sing.
*   it's the only way they can let it out.*

IF YOU LISTEN CLOSE, GRIEF WILL ALWAYS SING YOUR NAME

girls of isolation
inspired by olivia gatwood's pandemic instagram

i never knew how to define my emptiness until she was forced to
be lonely.
she is the darkness at the bottom of the boxes i've been
unpacking in isolation.
she is a pair of suffocating lungs behind a homemade mask.

but she is also beautiful.
she is creating universes from all this lonely. exploring them with
all the undone parts of herself.
my emptiness has left so much space for me.
and i am learning
the consequences
of what it means
to fill.

heavy

i've learned how to carry the world
on my shoulders.
i've figured out how to lift others up
with a straight spine
and a tucked chin,
taught myself how to hold baggage with calloused palms.

i feel like atlas
using my arms to bear the weight of sadness
and my legs to support the
pressure of my breath,

you could see me from a mile away.
not from the load i am carrying,
but the way in which i carry.

i stand tall.
my arms do not tremble
and my legs do not shake

and while i am strong enough to bear these burdens,

> *i think what i'm trying to say is*
> *everything feels so fucking heavy.*

the first time someone i knew died by suicide,
i was 15.

i stuffed my pockets full of blood-covered shell casings
and wondered if a bullet would
feel any remorse
if they knew they were
biting the hand that fed them;

i neatly folded suicide notes into paper cranes.
placed them at the bottom of my bag
where they were crushed and forgotten—
       underneath this weight, i am feeling
         crushed and forgotten—
i close my eyes.
i wonder if he would've ended his life
if he'd known he was
not the only one
tasked with carrying burdens.

years later, my husband has carefully peeled this baggage off my
shoulders to
relieve pressure from my spine.

he puts them on his back and calls it "sharing,"
       i see it and call myself "a burden."

and what a paradox it is
to carry the weight of the world
and still believe i am not needed.

i am tired of feeling this heaviness
inside and out
and now i'm wondering if there's a way

i can feel good inside without
using my end as a way out.

today, i let myself unpack
for the first time in years.
at the bottom of my bag,
i found old suicide notes that read
            i am tired of feeling this way.

i threw them away.

the best way to feel lighter
is to lighten the fucking load.

<u>these sirens sound like lullabies</u>

i like to compare my depression to war.
it is gruesome
and messy
and ruthless
and wicked,

but soldiers don't tell you
some wars can last
long after the echo of the last bullet fades.
some wars will uproot you from your home, and
make battlegrounds feel like safe spaces.

some wars will make you forget
you ever once knew the feeling
of refuge.

most times you'll never
feel at home
again.

transient

what they don't tell you about war is that it turns you into a ghost before you can even meet the enemy. that you will haunt every living thing that has ever loved you. they don't tell you the anticipation of the battle can make you seasick. that the moment you walk into the fight, you are an abandoned church. that there is no salvation for a savior.

my father returned from korea on a night i did not bother to remember. he must've said he loved me a million times, but to this day i've never trusted a stranger who was kind to me. i wanted to tell him i watched my mother become a widow every time she wrote a letter to a man who wasn't there to love her back. that all i was in his house was a prisoner of war. that i could never call our home a safe space when a soldier was sleeping in the room across the hall.

what they do tell you about war, though, is that it's for the greater good. that everything you love will be safe for another day if you keep a strong defense. if you can still get up with broken ankles. if you are willing to give your life for a fight that's not yours.

my father missed 5 birthdays. that is his struggle and my antebellum. i've learned that loving a man who always leaves has not made me a patriot. it has made me a renegade. it has made me weak from carrying the belief that i can only love someone that's within an arm's distance. it has made me understand that when it is time for a homecoming, you will never stop unpacking the baggage.

what if i don't
like what i find
when i unpack all
of this?

my sister turns 20 this month

and i think about how i wrote the letter **19** days ago.
i told myself i would put all **18** of my cousins in my will, but
there's not much of me to leave behind anymore.
my mom would always have that picture of me from prom when i
pretended to be happy at **17**.
i know it would only take **16** pills for it to work so i don't know
why i've been shaking the last **15** seconds.
i can name **14** reasons why i should throw the rest of the bottle
out the window,
but i can't. i can't do anything.
i wonder if my partner will still buy me tulips on my birthday
every **13**th of july.
if they would play all **12** songs on my favorite album just to
think of the way i used to sing after a long day of loving them.
but i can't think about that.
i made it to the **11**th hour and i'm calling it a day.
all **10** of my fingers are exhausted from gripping onto life this
hard.
there are probably still scratch marks inside of my mother from
the **9** months it took for me to become this hollow.
i hope my psychiatrist feels bad for the **8** different prescriptions
he wrote to numb me.
i really tried taking them all **7** days of the week but what
difference does **6** doses make when you're **5** minutes away from
goodbye.
i look out the window and think about how there are **4** cardinal
directions and yet i've never been able to find my way home.
i've tried to go **3** times before, but i can tell this is the day i won't
see the moon rise.

i close my **2** eyes to find the last thing i'm feeling.

and right now, i am sad that on my sister's birthday,
she will have **1** less plate to make at the dinner table.

do you believe in heaven?

yesterday, i came home to see god
sitting in my favorite chair. i said nothing.
i've known god all my life,
and he has a tendency to wander into spaces he shouldn't. when
i'm smoking. crying.
fucking. and i'm tired of him being so greedy,
wanting me to notice him. he is no more real than a cloud in the
sky. something to see but fall right through.

       i am here because i need a place to rest,
he says.

       we have met so many times now, that
       home is wherever you are.

i hate this because i am not a holy church.
and i can see why he's really here.
god has never had a home.
heaven is the place we dream about when the water gets too high.
the place we think we'll have when there's nothing left.

god isn't real and neither is his palace.
there is no place to rest anywhere in this existence.

we can only hope there is something more.

<u>her name is depression</u>

and she treated me better than any lover.
she ran her fingers through my hair
and took the air out of my lungs,

slowly,

until she left me breathless.

i loved her
even when she pushed me to the edge.

such a sweet talker.
such a nice dancer.
such a good kisser.

depression never wanted to lose me.
she only wanted me to lose myself.

I HAVE WRITTEN SO MANY POEMS ABOUT TAKING MY OWN LIFE THAT I DON'T REMEMBER HOW IT FEELS TO WRITE SOMETHING OTHER THAN A SUICIDE NOTE

help me

save me

why me

help me

save me

it hasn't gotten better

i wish people would stop saying it gets better.
even if it did, i would still have scars from all the fights my head
had with my heart.
even if it did, i wouldn't recognize myself.
the sad knows me better than my mother does.
the sad has been my most reliable friend.
i don't remember a time when i wasn't running toward the end
of the tunnel, only to find the light was from a star that died
lifetimes ago.

so, no. it doesn't feel like it gets better.
it feels heavier with every step.
i can hear my heartbeat echo off my bones
through this body i've abandoned.

it hasn't gotten any better,
but please,
tell me it won't get any worse.

home

my body looks like
a dirt road map
and i wish
i could use my hands
to navigate through
my thick skin
into my bones

i am tired of
missing the way it used to feel
to come home

<u>if i'm being honest</u>

i know suicide the way you know your first love. *not the romance,
the pain.* the never-fucking-ending pain that comes with
yearning. i have never wanted anything more than i want suicide.
and that scares me. i don't want to wake up one day to realize
i have been a killer my whole life. something to be afraid of.
something that knows no mercy. i wish i knew the definition of
ending did not have to be synonymous with goodbye. but here i
am. i'm sick in the same way you fear for your grandmother. this
depression is a crippling cancer with no name. i do not want to
want her anymore.

all i want is some quiet.

<u>too black</u>

being the color of
soil has never made
any flowers want to
take root in me.

i am still fighting
to prove that i can
grow rainforests with
just one seed and

i cannot wait
until i convince you
it is safe here.

am i next?

i kick my feet up onto my **black** couch and wonder how it got to
be that way. so dark, like it could hold entire galaxies—

and suddenly my legs are gone. they've blended into the couch.
and i am reminded i, too, am galaxy-holder, am sun-soaker,
am human, human, human—but this is not the way i am seen
through alabaster glasses. the earth reminds me i will never be
queen, only the **black** dirt she walks on. i'll never be a sister,
only suspect. i will never be human, human, human, only **black,
black, black**—

so on days i feel more couch cushion than outer space i will
remind myself my **black**ness is what makes me whole. my **black**
is the same color as the gun they shoot us with. my **black** gives
and it takes. my **black** will be with me at the end of a long walk
home. a run. a drive. a nap. my **black** is here, is here, is here. and
i will wear it so fucking loudly.

red blood

trying to explain self-harm to someone who's never self-harmed
before is like
trying to explain that racism still exists.

when you bring up this topic, a person will get visibly
uncomfortable and say things like:

> *i've never seen anything like this*

or

> *maybe don't act that way*

or

> *it's not like people have died from that*

but i line my wrists
the same way my ancestors would
line up in front of the cops and take beatings

i take beatings from myself because i do not feel good enough
i beat myself up because i am not good enough

but the difference between self-harm and racism is that
my blood runs a little bit darker than the color of your maga hats,

and unlike racism, i know when to stop.
and this is not me trying to glorify or justify self-harm.
i have tried for years to rationalize my belief that my arms
could not exist without cuts on them
that i am not myself unless i am bleeding
that if i am not punishing myself by cutting,

how else can i get the hate out,
because what good is a martyr
that has not bled,
as if i am taking the screams of every depressed person and
pushing them down onto my wrists.

one time a boy i liked said,
you're cool, but you're black. my parents would kill me if we
dated.
as if i am a scar on lady liberty's wrist,
meant to be hidden.

my brown skin leaves people with a burnt taste in their mouth
and my scarred wrists leave people with the smell of iron in their
lungs and

when i try to explain to you
i am cutting because i am hurting
and
when i try to explain to you
sometimes being black feels more like a curse than a blessing

you do not do anything but look at me, dressed in red, and say
"get over it"

as if the feeling of depression luring me in
and the taste of gunpowder on my lips is something i can "get
over."

i have been cutting since i was 15 and
i have been black since i was born.
you would think by 25 i would know how to

live with the feeling of
burning stares and stinging wrists.

this probably doesn't help.
i wish i could explain self-harm in a way that didn't make me
sound like i was trying to fight for something good

but maybe there's something about the way
my scars heal in white lines that
makes me think being covered would
finally make you
accept my skin.

<u>when our skin is too much</u>

my husband is a black man.

he is beautiful
and dark-skinned
and puts the earth's soil to shame—
not because his melanin is darker than the ground,
but because he is better than mother nature at growing beautiful
things
from his pores

and this is not to say he's perfect.
black culture taught him the best way
to deal with trauma was to bury it down like seeds,
and those seeds are still very much alive,
sprouting and rooting through his veins
and making him into a growing living thing,

this is to say i'm afraid for him.

i had a dream that one day,
men dressed in blue came to our garden.
they yelled, *all lives matter*
as they planted mines into the earth,
created earthquakes through the ground,
uprooting everything in the land trying to
bloom,

this is to say i am scared of cops.
afraid one day i'll get a call

saying my husband's melanin was too
dark for the cops to see where they were
going,
too dark for the cops to see the bruising,
too dark for the cops to see all he was trying to do
was shine.

my biggest fear is that i will become a black widow.
that i will have to take my husband's blood and mark myself with
red,

a scarlet letter and a warning that i will devour the weak things
around me.

a black widow is not seen as a black queen.
we are feared and not worshipped,
everyone tries to crush our homes instead of
giving us support

and i look at my black husband.
i wonder if i am already a widow.
already so scared of his death
i am covering myself in web,
wondering if these cops fear a black queen so much
that they are hell-bent on taking her king,

this is to say i love my husband.
there will not be a day where i don't tell him
to stay safe,
because there are men out there with tools
who will stop at nothing to kill your growth.

this is to say my husband is a black man.
his melanin is more night sky than black hole
and as king and queen we will create constellations
that litter your sky and remind you
beautiful things come from the dark.

this is to say i am not afraid.
and we will continue to grow.

<u>the one in which i am lynched</u>

when i hear my lover say
nigga,
i think of how my bloodline has always turned grief to gospel.
when
niggers
died,
niggas
made sure they mama was safe.
niggas
know we ain't never really been safe. // all my demons have
blue eyes. they have been attached to our veins since my great-
grandmother tried to scrub the black off her hands into the sink.
if god is real, blessed be the shackles he used to make us wanted.
i will never say he's merciful for taking them off when we begged.
// we knew abuse by the name of father. now i'm the
nigga
who wonders if i can't hear his voice because i don't sing the
hymns anymore. the
nigga
who has been pinned down and fucked to submission 'cause i
didn't wanna get on my knees for a master. the
nigga
who thinks every 10pm phone call will be my father's eulogy. the
nigga
that sees
niggas
drop on tv every other day. the
nigga
that thinks we have never recovered from the damage of having to

choose between killing ourselves and being killed. // we tell our
children generational curses can only be broken with an offering.
we will never be free if we keep passing the trauma down like a
rusty locket. //

niggas

can only take so much before our will starts to sound like a
suicide note. before it's easier to hang the rope ourselves.
before we invite the demons to cheer us on. before we feel safer
stepping off the chair than we did seeing the world standing on
top of it. before we become

just

another–

haiku: searching

i'm slowly breaking.
i can't find a way to stay;
let me out of here.

<u>dead ends</u>

i don't know who i'm supposed to be by now.
my whole life i've been full-speed down a highway with no exits.
wondering how no one is here to help me find a path that doesn't
lead to a dead end.
and through it all, i just want to know i mean something.
that if i drove off the edge of the earth, someone would look for
me in the stars.
i want to know i didn't leave burn marks on the lives i touched.
that i didn't waste time trying to leave a footprint running after
my dreams.
that what i do leave behind will tell the story of a lost heart who
wanted to be something more than a ghost.

i want everyone to know that i tried.
that my existence was noticed.
that my purpose in this universe wasn't just to be another person
who was forgotten in the midst of it all.

<u>winter</u>

for years i have
tried to make fires with
my heart but
have been too numb
to strike a match
on this paper skin.

i cannot wait
for this winter
to end.

<u>when you left</u>

you never know how you're going to feel when someone kills themselves.

i still remember his smile.
his laugh blended into the murmur of the
high school cafeteria
and three days later,
he shot himself.

a shotgun is an awfully loud way to say goodbye.
i wonder if he'd been screaming it long before he went,

like the boy who cried help
shouting to the villagers about the beast.
the neighbors were fooled by his gentle smile
and his warm words and decided
there was no way a wolf could be living in his mind.

you never know how you're going to feel when someone you know kills themselves.

i never met the second boy, but at 7:57am
his gunshot echoed through the halls.

and if a boy falls in the middle of the school
and everyone was there to hear it
who is at fault for not catching him?

*you never know how you're going to feel
when you try to kill yourself.*

i never really knew myself.
a hollow book of a girl leftover:
two parts suicidal,
one part terrified.

my screams did not come out of the barrel of a gun,
but instead through the rattle of a pill bottle.

i don't remember how many i took
but my heart was 500 pounds.
it feels wrong to live
but it felt worse to die.

suicide doesn't take away your pain,
it wraps it up in newspapers headlined with your ache
and hand-delivers what's left to your family
it's a story they will never forget.

if you aren't alive you will not feel the pain stop.
but if you stay, you will feel it shift.
there is nothing in this life
that lasts forever.

why did you go

you left without goodbye.
i don't know why you decided to go

and i don't think there's
anything left to say.

life gives,
then it takes.

and you were no exception.

<u>stay with me</u>

the ocean takes up
so much space.
i want to be seen
the way she is.

i want to feel full.
i want to sink ships
and still be seen as
the safest home on earth
despite the wreckage.

i may have
arms of sweeping
riptides, but

i do not mean to steal you
away.

i do not mean to drown you, either.

i just don't want to be alone
anymore.

empty

hollowness has a name.
her emptiness fills you up
and makes you believe
you cannot be whole
without her,

she is an echo.
you will whisper her name
and only get pain
in response,

you are enough
for her.
she cannot live
without your body to
carry her void

but she is too much for you.
open up.
let her go.

<u>mortician</u>

planning for the end
takes dirty fingernails and
scraped knees.

it is not a tidy act
to prepare the dead.

I buried my hope
somewhere out of reach
so i'm sorry
if you have to
dig a little to
find me

<u>overdose</u>

there's a moment during an overdose
when you get nauseous.
a moment when you choose to:
- throw up the fucking pills, or
- wash down the misery.

so i swallowed my spit.
gargled my pain.
pushed the dark things down my throat.

depression will take everything from you until it takes your life.

and i don't think people understand
most days
you cannot see yourself as one day older,
you cannot hear someone screaming "stay."

depression will take everything from you until it takes your life.

and you have to fight it back if you want to live.

you have to let your body
prove you are both the fire
and the ashes,
prove you could be both broken
and still beautiful,

and the best part about seeing my body as separate from my mind
was realizing

i was not my depression.

the next morning,
i woke up.

i looked over and saw the light
reflect off the floating dust
and thought
>   *the light is there,*
>   *i just have to trust it to find me.*

permanent

my fingertips do not know
the difference between scar
and skin

as if i have always been healing
as if part of me has always been
broken

and i promise to be gentle
and let myself feel the
mountains and valleys

of scar and skin
until i know it is all
still
me

breaking

it takes all i have
not to crumble.
days fall away
from my pores and i
no longer know the difference
between a summer moon
and a winter sun,
so today i'll lie in the wreckage.
make mountains out of the
parts that are growing
and hope today
will feel like a battle
i will be able to fight.

the climb will hurt, but i won't let you fall.

<u>suicidal girl</u>

when you picture a suicidal girl
you picture the color black.
you see her scars before you see her eyes
and wonder if she's ever known a life
where untouched skin
felt more like home
than scar tissue.

you wonder why.
how a girl who has the muscles
to smile
uses them to cry instead,

so, you don't pity her.
suicidal girls, after all,
are selfish.
they think of themselves
before they think of you,

and now you're questioning,
why am i even thinking of the suicidal girl
if she doesn't care for me?

i was 15 when the sky fell.
the view became the same with my eyes closed,
just dark,
and even with my eyes open
everything seemed so blurry.

i don't know how to describe the haze.
the constant welling of tears
were like contacts with the wrong prescription

or like how you can still see the sky after a fire
but the smoke makes the sunrays fight a little bit harder to shine
through.

you know honestly,
i hate metaphors for depression.
there is no great way to say
"i want to die."
there is no poetry to describe how i feel like
there is a hole in my chest
no amount of love could fill,

and people have tried.
they reach toward me
and think they're getting to me
but they're only going through me,
soaring through my open wounds
and waiting for me on the other side
where the grass is greener
and the sky is clearer

but i'm good at looking like a happy girl.

because when you picture a suicidal girl,
you do not see smiles and floral print.
you do not see me.

you don't see how i've spent the last 30 minutes covering my
scars with makeup because happy girls don't show the places
where they've bled.
you don't see the nights i spend clutching a phone in one hand
and a pill bottle in the other.
you don't see me in the bathroom on my lunch break, digging my
nails into my
thigh under my dress.

i am not a happy girl.
i am a suicidal girl.
and we are not selfish
or uncaring
or made of scar tissue and saltwater.
we are tired.
we think of your lasting presence more than we think of our
pending absence,
we think about the home we've built out of scars and
keep flooding it with our oceans.

when you think of a suicidal girl,
don't think.
open your arms and pull us in.
breathe into us because
god, we are so tired of doing the breathing.
run your fingers through our hair and remind us
sometimes touch is more necessity than desire.

and next time you picture a suicidal girl,
picture me.

paper cuts

it feels cold
like an ice water.
and honestly,
lines are never neat.
they're mismatched and crisscrossed
and never seem to fit.

the act of carving
never feels like thanksgiving.
i never feel full
and i never want to quit.

i don't know when the color red
stopped meaning love
and became something else.

i'm sorry for the mess.

silence

depression does not know the
definition of quiet.

my voice is gone and
the cries are here to stay.
all i am begging for
is some silence.

<u>sky</u>

maybe home is less this body
and more the world around it.
maybe i'll learn how to exist
without being all of it.

<u>i've taken my last breath three times before</u>
after the fray

1. the night before prom. pill bottles look like pez dispensers
   when you're hungry enough. goodbyes aren't sad if you see
   them coming. my mom woke me up the morning after to go
   to lowe's. *inhale.*
2. the night after church. forgive me father for i have no way
   out of my mind. hands shake when you don't believe in what
   you're praying for. my tongue has never looked so white. my
   alarm woke me up for school in the morning. *inhale.*
3. the night after class. they never tell you that college is
   as lonely as it is full. i collected pills like they were state
   quarters. and i spent them fast. my roommate woke me up
   in the morning with a smile on her face. i've never felt more
   tired. *inhale.*

BREATHING COMES IN PAIRS, EXCEPT FOR TWICE:

ONE BEGINS, AND ONE'S GOODBYE.

—THE FRAY, ENOUGH FOR NOW

<u>and when the choir sings</u>

my voice is a moonrise wave,
reminding me i am big when i
am supposed to be.

my body is made holy.
hands rise and fall around my
skin and
this is called baptism.

my toes find my feet find the floor
and i call this grounding.

i have never believed in
blessed things
and yet
i am
becoming something called
righteous.
godly.
scripture.

and when the choir sings,
i am made church.

healing and the grace that comes from it

(i can't believe that i made something out of all of this.)

<u>haiku: awake</u>

now, i am undone
i have burst at the seams and
i'm becoming new

<u>better</u>

i get out of bed
this morning.
my hands find themselves
to be keys,
floating down to meet my ankles
and unlocking the anchors that
hold me at sea,
i make my way to the bathroom.
i wipe the sleep from my eyes
and look at the portrait in the mirror.

i see the sun climb through the window.
it feels warmer today.

the one in which my sorrow is disguised as a self-portrait

i look at my past through rose-colored glasses.

my yesterdays have never felt traumatic. it was a neighborhood garden overflowing with posies. i was a fanny-packed tourist with camera-lens eyes.

i thought the world was magnetic, the way i would be pulled to sea at the sigh of the sunset breeze. but eventually i was always left shipwrecked in the middle of the tide.

so it's no wonder i am as tumultuous as a hurricane. i have been crawling to land and spitting up saltwater ever since i learned the word "drown." my swimmer's ear makes every "i love you" sound like a tornado siren. i have been spiraling just to conjure something worth feeling.

in the end, i return to the garden to find my toes sink into my grandmother's front lawn. i walk through the front door and find another pair of rose-colored glasses sitting on the coffee table. i put them on and see a picture of me hanging crooked on the wall.

my cheeks have never looked so rosy.

who
are you?
who
do you
want to be?

treatment

i haven't been writing much lately because
i've been in treatment.
in august i held a razor in one hand and a pill bottle in the other
and wondered if
for once i could make a suicide note sound like a poem
but it's not often
goodbyes sound like metaphors
so instead
i was admitted into treatment.
when you're in an intensive outpatient program,
most people tend to think you're okay because
you can sleep in your own bed at night and you don't have
to wait for the hospital to help you to breathe
because they trust you to do the breathing on your own.
but being on life support isn't always having tubes forced down
your throat.
sometimes life support looks like pill calendars and dbt
worksheets and electric razors
>   *(because you can't trust yourself with*
>   *the normal ones)*
sometimes life support looks like 4 hours of therapy a day, and
itchy scabs, and wishing you could chase down sleeping pills with
a bottle of wine
>   *(but knowing that would get you kicked*
>   *out of the program)*
sometimes life support feels less like machines forcing your
lungs to breathe, and more like therapists forcing your limbs to
stand.

i met a girl named kate. we talked about how we tend to pour all
of our worth into people who don't deserve it and she said,
      maybe we put all of our worth into
      others because then, at least we can
      actually see that our worth exists.

and i wonder, if we are only living to make our existence known.
i wonder, if each failed attempt hurts so much because it reminds
us that we will never truly feel known.
i wonder, if i have a hard time getting off life support because i
do not know what it feels like to just exist.
i wonder, why does it hurt so much to be reminded that we exist—

i wanted treatment to cure me. i wanted to walk out, fist high in
the air, screaming *fuck you* to my depression but instead,

i sat in my car. i played with the keychain they gave me as a token
for completing the program.

i let myself breathe. without the tubes. without the machines. i
let my lungs exist,
and for the first time in seven weeks
or seven months
or seven years
i did not want to stop existing

and not feeling suicidal isn't as dramatic as i thought it would
be—
it turns out,
not feeling suicidal feels a lot like wanting to see your husband's
face as soon as you get off work.
not feeling suicidal is loving the taste of the office coffee, even

after it gets stale.
not feeling suicidal is saying i love you, and knowing they mean it
when they say i love you back.
i let myself shave yesterday.
and for once,
i did not see the razors as a way out
~~(but as a way to get the goddamn hair off my legs)~~.

i love being off life support.
i still feel my depression sitting on my chest every day telling me
to leave but now,
i love that i can tell her:

not today.

the truth we bury

this life is worth it.
and i know you don't believe it.
you've been pushed down so much that living brings you lower
than the earth's gravity ever could.
but there will be a day when things feel lighter. when you will
look up and the clouds will part. when the sun won't burn.
it is never too late for you to be loved in the way you deserve.
for each scar you have, there is someone waiting to help it fade.
to hold you close until you remember what warmth feels like.
to fill your cup after being empty for so long.
and you will find a reason to keep going.
even the ocean returns to stillness after a hurricane.
there is no amount of destruction that you can't return from.
you are worth the rebuilding.
you are more than what drowns you.
you will survive through this storm.

linguistics
after caitlin conlon

in a language that doesn't have the word "love," i say, "i took the dog out this morning so you could sleep in." i say, "i'm going to tell you how i'm feeling the best way i can." i say, "i didn't relapse today." i say, "i went to therapy." i say, "please, *please* don't leave me." i say, "i know i'm not living for you but, god, i'm so glad i'm living for us." i say, "your mom called yesterday asking if i was okay." i say, "i don't know if i'm ever okay but i woke up to you this morning." i say, "i am trying so fucking hard to keep sight of the light." i say, "i am still here," i say, "i am still here," i say, "i am still here."

womanhood

and with that,
she ended wars and
created flowerbeds from
old bullet casings and
statues erupted in her name,
and the churches echoed
with the sounds of prayers
to hold her up.
her sisters stitched her cuts
and wiped her tears.

she has made everything
around you
home.

and you should be grateful.

you're meant to be here

the sun wiggles its
way through the window
as a reminder
the light will always return
in the morning.

<u>i think about ending my life—</u>

and then i think about how
you would still love me even if i weren't here tomorrow.

and i think of endless tomorrows
of being loved by you

and with you,
i'm closer to infinity than i'd ever be
in the ground.

so i'll stay.
and i'll wait—

for tomorrow.

a ballad of yesterdays
after ari eastman

i leave the tv on just to be held by the static.
it's the closest thing i have to the hum of my high school gym
winter formal.
the echo of our teenage selves laughing off rooftops.
the choke that comes with goodbyes.

i have never been good at growing older.
there is too much pain in acknowledging the silence that comes
with it.
i want to be 17 again, driving down the highway with everyone
i've ever loved.
the windows down, singing our favorite song.
knowing there is no loneliness in harmony.

we're all each other's background noise these days.
we close our eyes and listen to the static that comes with fading
out.
we remember what it was like when it was so,
so piercing.
we learn how to be okay with the way
things will never be the same again.

<u>friendship</u>

hold my hand.
remind me that trauma
is not meant to be felt
alone.
that pushing the thoughts back
will cause nothing but sore arms
and bleeding wrists:
comfort me.
tell me i am strong enough
to hold this in
and strong enough to
let this out,

be my friend.

36.1156°N
97.0584°W

It wasn't home
but it was the
closest thing I
ever had.

<u>when it feels too much</u>

if it gets too heavy,
remind the earth of your footprint.
dig it into the soil
so deep
that mother nature holds your ankles
with her roots;
be still.
the wind is here to uplift you
not uproot you
and on this solid ground,
square your shoulders,
raise your arms,
and hold.

what i mean when i say "open up"

today my dentist told me to unclench my jaw
and suddenly i am back in your bedroom,
listening to you beg me to open up more.

and i've never been good at softening
enough to let people in.
my chest is scored from all the people
who have tried to get through to me.
and i don't mean to be like this.
truth be told, i want to tell you i love you so much that i feel the
numbness in my hands start to thaw when you hold me.
i love you so much that i can feel your heartbeat through my
fingertips.
when you say my name, i come alive
in a way that makes me wonder how
i was a ghost for so long.
how i was able to live alone
in this body i call home.
how the windows and doors have been bolted shut all this time.
i am trying to wrench them open but i'm scared you'll leave as
soon as i do.
that you'll hate what's inside.
that when you walk away
you'll bring the floodwaters.
that i'll drown because i peeled back every layer for you.

i'm learning it hurts more
to clench my jaw than it does to let go.
i'm scared you will hurt me when i open up

but i am trying to give
you more space
to love me.

<u>unwind</u>

tangle yourself up
in the threads of
my veins,

follow them all the
way to my heart and
unravel me.

cut away the pieces
that are too knotted
to let blood flow and
allow me to bleed out my
sorrows until
i am empty.

refill me until
i am too full to
feel anything

and help me redefine
what it means
to be lost inside
myself.

<u>sunlight</u>

there's lots of light
today.
it's flooding in my pores and
filling me up and
i hope more days start to feel like
the sun.

bridges

i am exactly where i need to be.
bridges have burned
and their ashes have left a trail
leading me to
right now,

and i am scared.
i don't know what it's like
to be so sure of anything that's
not an ending

so i'll sit in the ashes.
form them into sandcastles and
call it my new home.

this is living, after all.

<u>poetry</u>

the poetry comes to me
in waves and
i am still searching for
the moon that moves me.

still wondering if it's
my trauma or depression
creating riptides inside
my veins.

i am finding ways to
cope with the ebb and flow.
i am rocking this boat instead
of drowning.
the sky doesn't look as
dark.

<u>night</u>

for you,
the night comes early.
you do not know the dawn,
only the darkness before it
because new days feel
like both a nightmare
and a daydream

but, you made it today.
you did not take your last
breath, despite
begging the moon to
grab it.

you are strong
because you are you.
and the rest doesn't matter.

a comprehensive list of feelings i never would've experienced if you kept loving me:

1. childlike joy. looking at the world and knowing it's mine, all mine to take. understanding that i am small and that is okay. one day soon i will be made big.
2. heart-wrenching sorrow. a dandelion is only a weed if you look at it, head tilted. i was afraid i was only beautiful because of you.
3. enough. i would've missed this feeling of being enough. of being both a candle lit from both ends and a flower falling down a hillside. something other than what i started as.
4. gratitude. i don't have much to say about this one. not much other than thank you for not loving me anymore. i can feel everything again.

new love

i don't believe in god
but i know the feeling
of christ's divinity.
i see angels when you
touch my scars.

you turn my dark places
into heaven's gates
and welcome me with forgiveness:

i've tried to play god by
taking my own life
and you have shown me
the power of mercy,

and i will love you
unconditionally.

<u>homecoming</u>

take me to
the parts of yourself
you call home
and tell me
i am welcome to
rest for a while

the garden that bursts with wanting

the easiest thing i ever did was picking you.

i know this sounds silly,
how out of a million beautiful things,
i was drawn to you,
but imagine the biggest garden you can,
and imagine yourself in it.
roots so deep even storms cannot lift you from the ground.
leaves that make the most beautiful song when the wind comes.
and i don't mind that you're not always blooming.
you open up when you're ready.
when it's safe.
when the world can handle your beautiful.

anyway, i always knew i'd love you.

you are so grounded that you laugh at gravity for thinking it's
holding you down.
you look toward the sun because you know that's how you grow.

and even though there are a million beautiful things around me,
i walked to the nearest garden i could find
and out of all of the flowers
i picked you.

an ode to pandemic friendships, or, *please wait for the meeting host to let you in*

as if i haven't already been welcomed in this shared home called grief.
as if i haven't already seen the way you don't blink when you talk about your father, a soft focus of trying to find the man you wanted him to be.
i see you trying to shrink. how a good meal sometimes feels treacherous.
how you can never find a beautiful way to disappear.
i know you would rather be alone.
love has no company that hasn't left you sitting at the door like your mother's bloodhound.
like a child wanting more from the father who could never give.

you ask for the password and i open my chest.
it is stuffed full of the pieces of the person i could never be.

somehow we are able to stitch our wounds.
you've helped me heal but i can't touch your hands.
i don't think we ever need to hold each other
to help carry our grief.

And what a joy it is to be alone but never lonely

dandelion

i told you i loved you and you said dandelions make you sick.
that there aren't enough wishes in the world to grow beautiful
from cracked soil,
so i sit there.
wilted.
wondering if i am no longer a flower
but just a weed.
spreading myself over anything
that will have me.
but then the wind calls me, and i float away.
i go across fields of broken, looking for a safe place to land
and i realize,
i was never a flower to you because you could never hold me
gently.
you could never love me wholly.
so i am here.
a dandelion with a stem that holds oceans.
i will bloom in the most wonderful places.

<u>a sad girl's guide to living</u>

it takes less than
seven minutes
to swallow a bottle
of pills,
to chase it down with
tears and jack.

it is incredible that
you can end your life
in less time than it takes
to come into it.

incredible that you can
count down your existence
with 500 heartbeats—

i hope you change your mind.
use those seven minutes to
swim to the edge of the sad,
not drown in it.

and let yourself live.
you've got time.

haiku: mantra

put yourself ahead
of everything stopping you
from being healthy

maps

become a cartographer.
make me the map
to your wildest dreams and
carve the way there with
your fingertips.

trace snowcapped mountains
and river-filled valleys
and do not stop until
you are home.

<u>juxtapose</u>

be both the hurricane and the shelter.
the sun and the moon.
the ship and the waves.
carry souls and protect hearts
but do not be afraid to take down
walls and burn bridges in
your wake.
you are soft and powerful.
and that is enough.

price tag

i hope you try to
stop making barcodes
on your wrists
and start seeing yourself
like gold.

priceless does not mean
you are worthless.

it means
you are everything.

welcome home

i treat my body like a graveyard.
i bury my dead things inside
and wait for the skeletons to
come out at night;
i always craved the
calm of endings,
until a daisy appeared.
she pushed through my soil
with fierce abandon,
spread roots through my bones
and placed petals where
thorns once loved:
she planted seeds in my home.
i am starting to grow.
this graveyard is starting to look
more like a church.
i can't wait to welcome her.

<u>to the ones who have tried to kill themselves:</u>

1. if you're reading this, your suicide attempt didn't work.
which isn't something you need me to remind you of because
i know you're very aware. and i'm sorry. not in the fucked-up
way like *i'm sorry you're not dead* or *i'm sorry you're alive*
but i'm sorry because i know how it feels to wake up every
morning and think *holy fuck, i can't even kill myself right.*

2. how are your doctor appointments going? because that's
what we have to call them to get excused at work, *"doctor
appointments"* because *"the psychiatrist"* doesn't have the
same innocent ring to it. are you taking your meds? how
many have you tried? sorry i'm so pushy, i just need to know
i'm not alone because i've been fed lexapro, pristiq, lamictal,
geodon, prozac, paxil, trazadone, latuda, vistaril, effexor,
and don't forget the lunesta to sleep; i'm asking because
trust me, i understand that being a cocktail of meds will
never make your head feel less like a molotov cocktail.

3. i remember when my parents found out. not that i was
suicidal, but that i tried to commit suicide. it was more
painful than my razor blades could ever be. my therapist
asked if i'd ever overdosed and i said yes. my dad said, *you
did?* and i said yes. and then we said nothing.

4. how many times have you tried to kill yourself? i hope only
one. i hope after you woke up so dizzy and full of dissolved
pills and vodka, your wrist sore from bleeding that you said
never again but i know that's probably not true. i know even
if you didn't try again, you wanted to try again and if you
didn't want to–*want to*–try again you're still not the same
as you were before swallowing the first pill and i'm sorry
because:

5. *it's your depression, not you*
6. *it's your depression, not you*
7. *it's your depression, not you*
8. if you ever decide you don't want to be here anymore, know that your disappearance will cause an echo of screams no one will ever stop hearing. and i know, *fuck everyone else. let me do one thing for myself. it doesn't matter if i'm gone* but let me tell you, yes. fuck everyone else. stay alive for you. do it to see your cuts turn to scars, do it to see your parents grow old, do it so that one day you can say *i fucking did it.* just do it.
9. it's been 6 years since my last attempt and i still itch for pill bottles every day. when it's impossible to breathe without feeling your depression sitting on your chest, sleep on your stomach. suffocate her so you can sleep for a night, and when she's back tomorrow, rinse and repeat. stay a little longer. i know it's hard. but i know it's worth it.

<u>memoir</u>

i did not expect you to be here.
i figured that by now, you'd be six feet deep, pushing daisies from
your earth-colored skin, but instead, you're here.
you're feeling the sun warm your shoulders,
but not letting it burn,
you can feel touch without letting it sting,
and who knew you could swim
without drowning?
i have always been afraid to admit
that i love you
because i feared it would make you want to stay,
but now i'm not afraid of commitment.

thank you for sticking around. i'm happy i'm getting to know you
better.

memoir (ii)

somehow you are both the ash and the phoenix.
the mud and the lotus.
the happy and the sad;
you are a juxtaposition.
you are both glass half full and half empty.
you are the winter sun and the summer moon.
you are both black and white,
yearning for grey,
yearning for some color in your life.
you are scared.
you don't know which way is best
and that is okay.
sit in the darkness and dance in the light.
understand you are both lost and found,
and it's okay if you don't know
where to return to;
you are here.
and i know it's hard.
but you are.
keep choosing to be.

i promise, one day it will be enough.

<u>recovery</u>

recovery is dancing to paramore in my bathroom until i break a sweat. recovery is getting in the shower and holding this body that keeps me. recovery is looking at this body and knowing its trauma. recovery is loving it anyway. recovery is knowing it's normal to be soft inside and out. recovery is not keeping the good things an arm's length away. recovery is not looking for my self-worth in an empty stomach. recovery is loving the girl that sits on her bathtub, out of breath in joy. recovery is loving myself. recovery is loving myself.

recovery (ii)

when it gets better
(and i promise, it'll get better)
you'll see daisies everywhere you step.

they'll lead you home.

the end

(we're here. we're here. we're here.)

paper girl and the knives that made her

she is tinder.
she has been ripped apart and
thrown into the fire
by wolves and razor blades.
her brain is a torn journal page.
her wrists are lined with the story of how
she survived.

she is paper.
make her into a paper crane.
a fortune-teller.
an origami heart.

release your wildest dreams onto her.
she can hold it all.
be gentle.
she is fragile.

she is the person i have always wanted to be.

I may be a
paper girl but
that just means I have
forests inside of me.

reader,

thank you for doing this with me. we fought through the feeling of holding our stories in our skin and being ripped apart by the knives that are trauma and depression.

reader, thank you for understanding that recovery is less highway and more dirt road. maps cannot quite find it but it's there, i swear, just keep looking.

i am better now. i am not always okay. you won't be either. but we can do our best to feel it all.

i know it is okay to be a paper girl.
and if we're careful enough,
our stories will live on forever.

you have a purpose.

ari b. cofer

acknowledgements

thank you to the readers who said this book was worth writing

thank you to my best friends for the years of love and poetry
you've given me

thank you to gerald, for loving and supporting me in the way that
i need

thank you to michelle and trista for the care they gave to paper
girl

and the final thanks goes to me,
because i am still here, and fighting,
and alive to share these stories.

about the author

ari b. cofer is a full-time writer, wife, and pet mom. while
her roots are in texas and oklahoma, she currently resides in
washington state. as a passionate mental health advocate, she is
dedicated to spreading awareness about mental health through
sharing her story and the stories of others.

ari can most likely be found walking to the beach, writing on her
patio, or on instagram @ari.b.cofer.